PROVIDENT HOSPITAL

Author's Note: Dr. Daniel Hale Williams established Provident Hospital to provide a safe place for African Americans to receive the best health care. It's also the place of my birth.

-K.C.D

This book belongs to

_____

Purchase other fun history books: www.createspace.com/3487864 or Amazon.com
Contact author: fun_history@juno.com

Twas the night of a miracle
When the doors opened wide,
In stepped new nurses
Wearing badges with pride.

The eager young nurses
Stood in a row,
With sparkling white dresses
And smiles all aglow.

Doctor Daniel Hale Williams
Arrived promptly at nine
To train the young nurses
That waited in line.

Doctor Williams taught stitching
With a needle and thread.
The mending stops bleeding
From your toes to your head.

They learned how to tell
A scalpel from a knife,
Knowing the difference
Can save someone's life.

He took wide bandages
And wrapped a dummy's limb.

Certificate of Achievement

In 1895 Dr. Daniel Hale Williams
Co-founded the
National Medical Association
for African American doctors

After he finished,
The nurses practiced on him.

He sat down for a moment
And listened to nurse Joan.
She held a dangling skeleton
And labeled every bone.

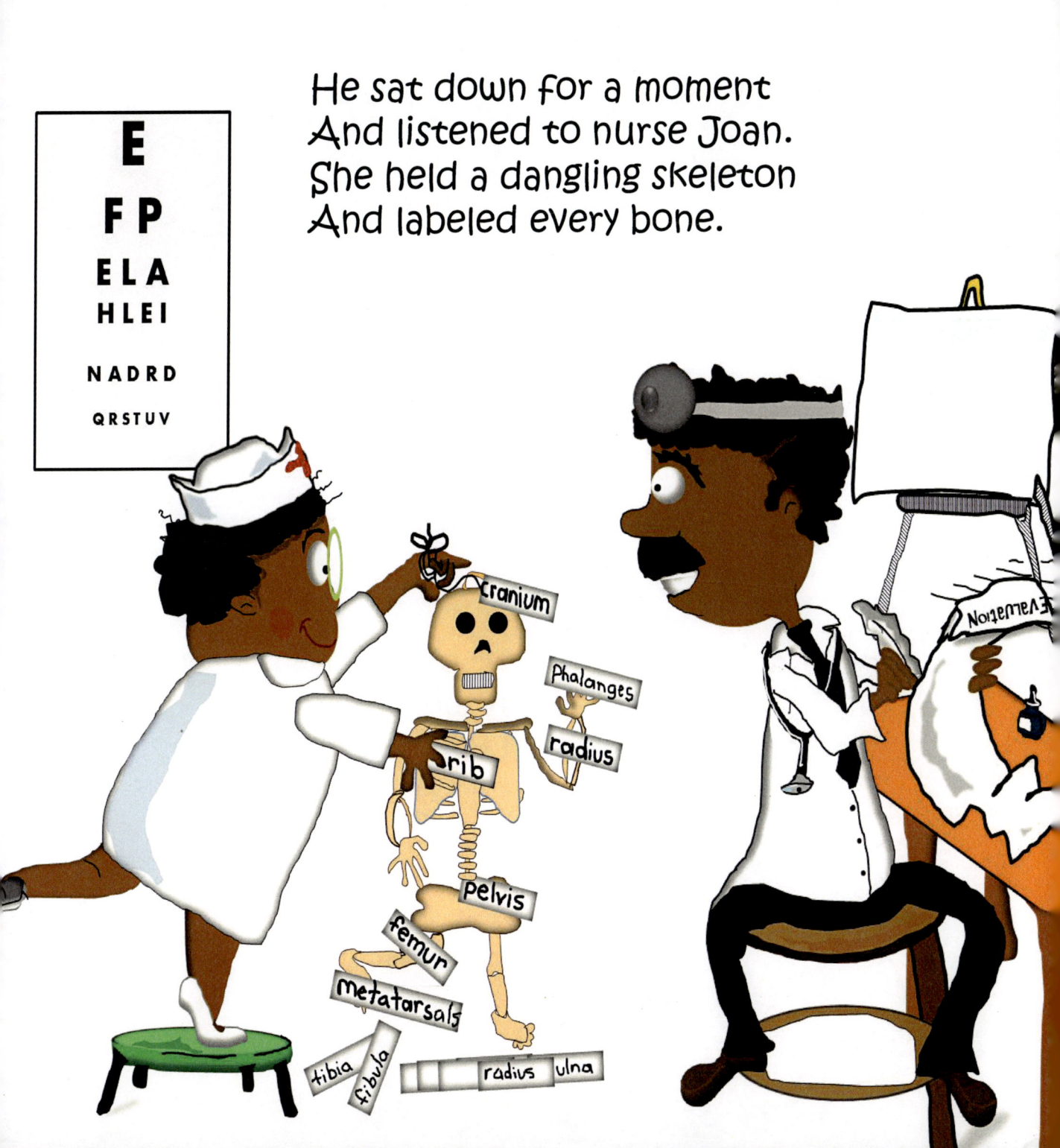

The nurses practiced on each other
and did it with zing.
Their zeal was utterly amazing.
They learned everything!

They hummed while they worked,

And they toiled with such care.

The look on their faces
Showed they wanted to be there.

Doctor Williams in his lab coat
And the nurses in white
Ceased their days' training
And gathered to say goodnight.

When all of a sudden,
Someone burst through the door.
He yelled, "A man is bleeding
And he's lying on the floor!"

Away they quickly dashed,
Like a football team.
The sight was so dreadful
A nurse let out a scream.

The poor man was stretched out
Blood oozed from his chest.
Everyone sadly feared
A night without rest.

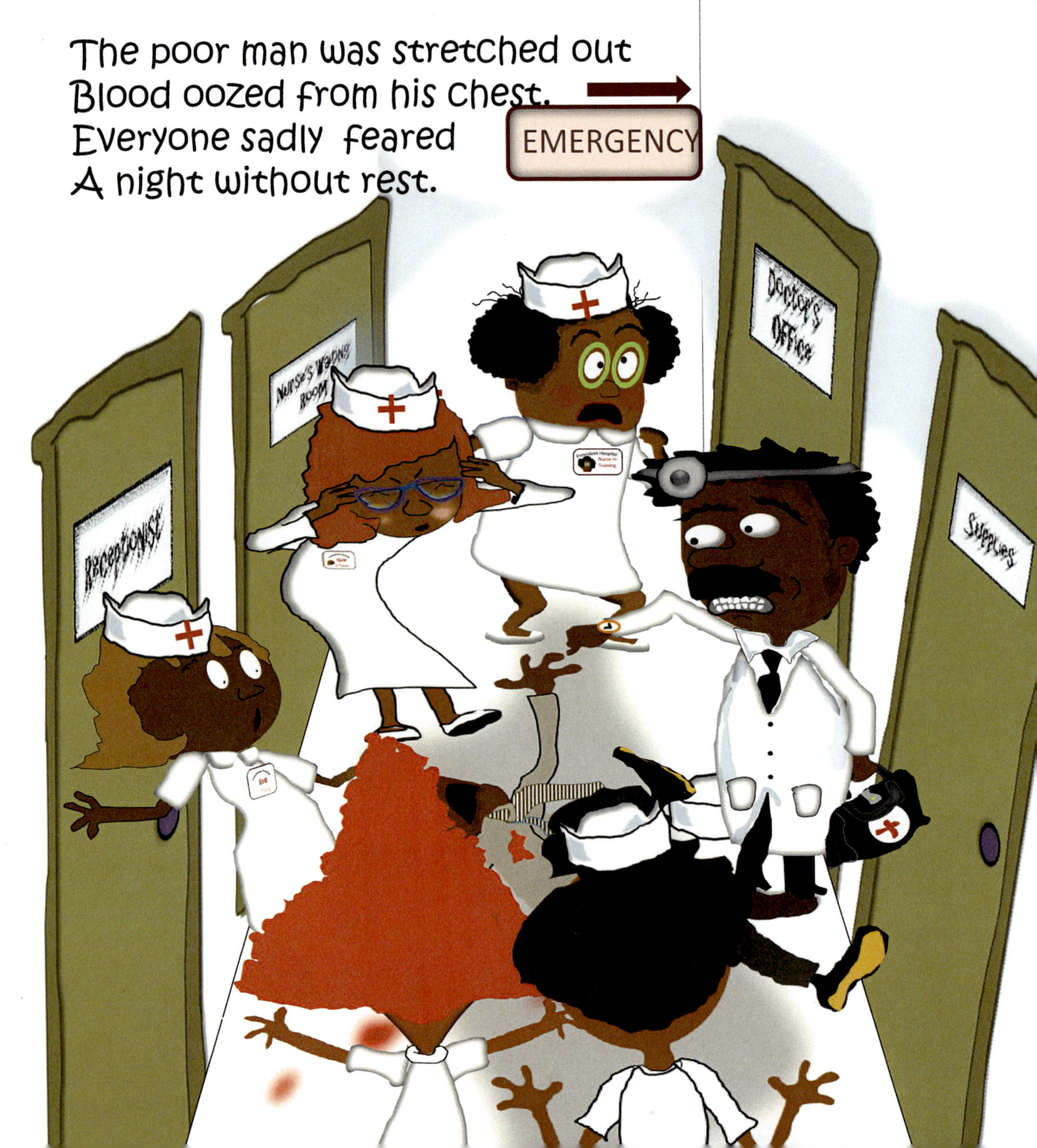

"Oh doctor," cried nurse Lynn
"What are we to do?
You have to make him well.
He's counting on you!"

Doctor Williams paced back and forth
And nervously scratched his head.
Then the sparkle in his eyes
Said there was nothing to dread.

WAITING ROOM

EMERGENCY ROOM →

Off to the operating room
The doctor and nurses flew.
Doctor Williams was quite sure
He'd know what to do.

With new uniforms and washed hands
Doctor Williams put them to the test.
"Just hand me the tools I ask for"
Was his urgent, no-nonsense request.

A nurse passed the scalpel
Without a delay.
Dr. Williams thanked her
And started cutting right away.

Then they gave him a sharp needle
With a long string of thread.
He bent over and began stitching
Without lifting his head.

When at last it was over,
Doctor Williams let out a sigh.
The patient's heart was restored.
It made the whole staff cry.

Then, without any warning,
Grins flashed on their faces.
They shook the doctor's hand
And gave warm embraces.

Several weeks thereafter,
From the bed the man rose.
He pulled off the covers
And put on his clothes.

The doctor's work was stupendous!
In fact, he was so smart
To be the very first doctor
To sew a torn heart.

Twas the night of a miracle,
Everyone would agree
Dr. Daniel Hale Williams
Would go down in history.

Made in the USA
San Bernardino, CA
01 February 2017